101 poems about Things We Should Be Loud About

101 poems about
Things We Should Be Loud About

Lindokuhle Mathenjwa

101 poems about Things We Should Be Loud About

info@rockhopperbooks.co.za | www.rockhopperbooks.co.za

Contents © Lindokuhle Mathenjwa

Illustrations © Lindokuhle Mathenjwa

Print ISBN: 978-0-7961-6399-8

Published in 2024 by Rockhopper Books

Printed by Digital Book Printers

All rights reserved. No part of this publication may be reproduced, stored in or introduced into a retrieval system, or transmitted, in any form, or by any means electronic, mechanical, photocopying, recording or otherwise, without the prior permission of the publisher. Any person who commits any unauthorised act in relation to this publication may be liable to criminal prosecution and civil claims for damages.

101 poems about Things We Should Be Loud About

Dad, this one's for you.

&

For all those too afraid to say he did it, she did it, or they did it.

I'll say it for you honey, louder than you could have ever imagined.

101 poems about Things We Should Be Loud About

101 poems about Things We Should Be Loud About

Here you go...

PREFACE..7
SILENT SHOUTS..9
LOUDER THAN WORDS.. 6
BREAKING THE MOULD... 113
REVELATIONS AND DECEPTIONS..........................147

101 poems about Things We Should Be Loud About

PREFACE

I'm sure there's been a point in time where you wanted to say something, but chose to keep quiet instead. The thought of each of those instances almost eats you up every time. Each moment you didn't fill the silence with words, every time your eyes filled up with tears and your heart boiled but, still, you kept your lips glued together. Whether it was to keep the peace or the idea that you can't put your feelings into words frustrates you, maybe you feel tired of constantly raising your voice but never being heard. Either way, your mind and mouth seem to shut down simultaneously. In some instances, you could have been afraid, or just simply had no strength, no courage, or thought that no one would believe you. Perhaps you felt that your words wouldn't make any sense, possibly even worse, you were told to keep your mouth shut, or else…

For all those times, my dear reader, for the times you should have been loud, for the times you should have had the courage, for the times you didn't want to, for the times you were told not to, for the times you chose to go cry alone in the unseen so you won't be heard. Just know I'm here to be loud. Loud about it all. Here to amplify the silenced thoughts and vomit the swallowed words. (Eww, how could you…?)

One thing for certain is that you picked this book, because you are tired of being on mute; well, so am I.

101 poems about Things We Should Be Loud About

1

SILENT SHOUTS
A Roar Against Social Injustice and Revolutionising Change

101 poems about Things We Should Be Loud About

101 poems about Things We Should Be Loud About

Be a being afraid of silence.

Be loud.

Be emotional.

Be passionate.

Be angry, but in control of your anger.

Be firm.

Be courageous.

Be consistent.

Be rigid with your words, but not rude.

Be truthful.

Be clear.

Be steadfast.

Be violent with your words, but not your hands.

Be considerate.

101 poems about Things We Should Be Loud About

Be intelligent.

Be wise.

Be a child to new things at times.

Be curious.

Be involved.

Be vigilant.

Be ambitious, but not ambiguous.

Be anything but silent.

- A calling to BE

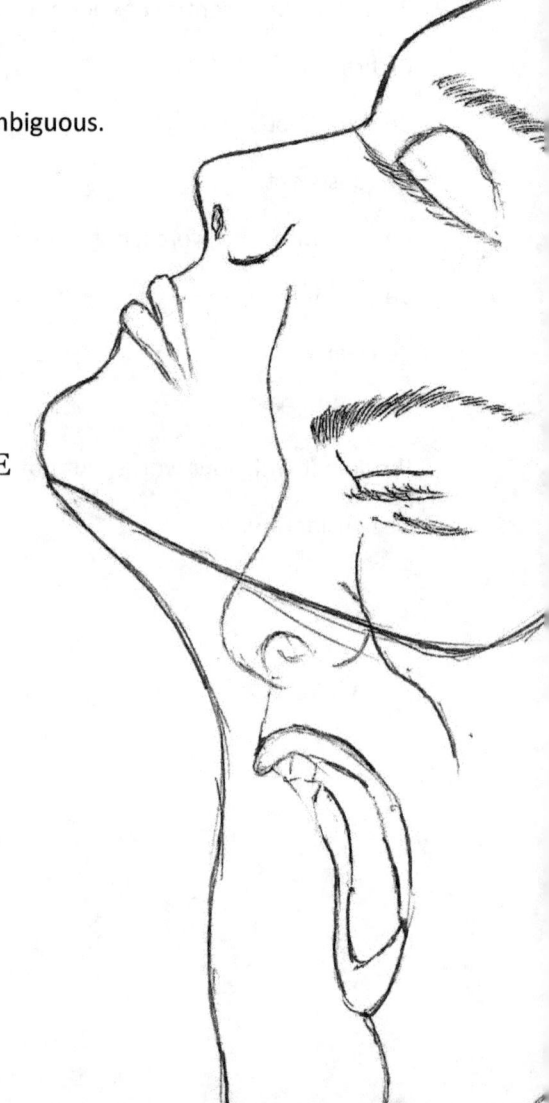

101 poems about Things We Should Be Loud About

Let us dive relentlessly into the mess,

And untangle history.

Let the stories of our ancestors

Who were powerful in body and mind

Not become a mystery,

Or a white-washed consistory.

We must claim victory.

On behalf of those before us,

On behalf of those ahead of us.

This is our burden.

As the people between the past and the future

We are the suture,

Amidst the wounds and incisions

Weary of every decision and aware of the mission

To be one as a people,

And forget race but remember the race

To fulfilment and equality

A dream above the horizon

A dream above the mountain,

A mountain we should all – together as one

Prepare to conquer.

- No Mysteries

It's revolting to watch

How intelligence

Is scaled by how western you sound.

How western you dress.

How western you live.

How western you behave.

It's not modern, no.

Its abandonment. Its control.

It's a race of how fast you can run from your roots

Because in this time

Our ways, our ancestral ways,

They're just too peculiar

If you share the same sentiments

You…

You're out of touch.

- Western Scale

Being black

Is occasional.

It happens

When you seldom visit

The mountains and valleys.

When the dowry gets paid.

When the baby is born.

When someone dies.

Then you cry and laugh while

Speaking the diluted version

Of your mother tongue.

And still, then,

You'll have to westernise

The occasion,

If not,

Did it ever happen?

- Occasionally Black

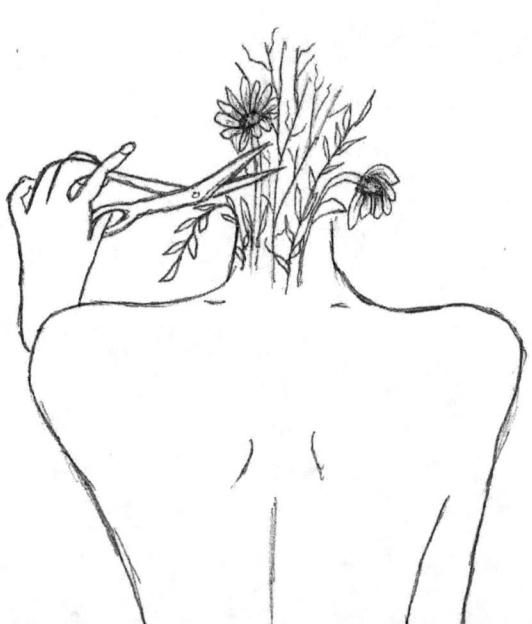

Though our hearts have been grazed

Our eyes must continue to gaze

At the promises we've made to ourselves

Come miles of grim road

And smoke from fires

We didn't start,

But found on the way

To conquer matters of misery.

We must remember there are

Still many miles that lie ahead.

- Matters of misery

There are people who've denied themselves sleep

For the sake of their dreams, For the sake of life,

For the sake of feeling worth it,

For the sake of God.

Those who cry behind the door

So others wouldn't be in awe

That rain falls from their eyes too.

Even though it sounds

101 poems about Things We Should Be Loud About

Too good to be true.

Too good to be bruised,

Too good to be…

For to be ungrateful

Is to lay your worries on your lips

And hook things you cannot

Change onto your heart

- The reason

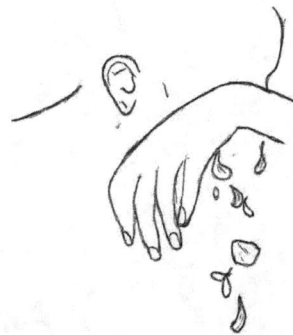

101 poems about Things We Should Be Loud About

You know stars shine truly

When all earth is dark, and few men are awake

For they know what is at stake.

Some are called to work

While some are called by the

Rumbling in their stomach.

Then some are called by defeat

And they heed the call

With yet another bottle,

Maybe in a brothel

Where the dead are living

In between now and then.

Feeling forgotten.

Feeling lost.

Feeling euphorically broken.

- Forced callings

Our minds have been polluted

To think that we need a crutch

To walk into success because

Hey, success is not black,

And if it is,

There has to be a little bit of white.

See, diversity is not a problem

To the middle class,

But the one percent, that percent is not diverse.

So why should we conform?

To the idea of a rainbow that is conditional,

A rainbow that only appears when it rains,

And If only you knew who makes it rain.

You'd believe me when I say

Our minds are polluted.

- The 1%

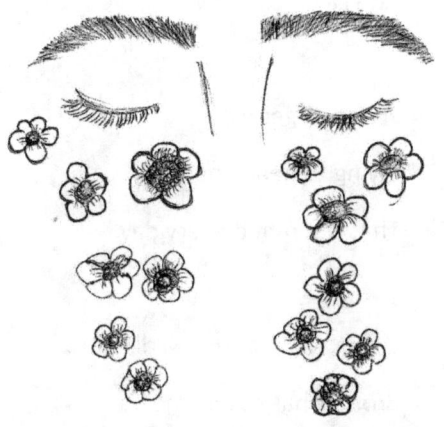

Are we that oblivious or

Have we just become

A numb nation?

Numb to indoctrination.

Numb to the mockery.

Numb to it all.

Hell, we go as far as to

Make fun of ourselves

And call it comedy.

Trying to get by,

Trying to heal wounds,

That is scraped every day.

When we hear how a distant

Brother has been

Shot and killed.

See I don't even need to continue

Because you already

Know who did it.

And in the eyes of men

Lies an unsettling fear.

Glancing from corner to corner,

Trying to find a place to hide

The imminent thought,

'If tomorrow ever comes'

Will he be jobless or lifeless?

Physically or mentally?

Because speaking truly,

Men are just holding

On by the thread,

If there's any tread left at all.

- Numb Nation

101 poems about Things We Should Be Loud About

We have been subconsciously

Engineered to hate ourselves,

To the extent of pure agony.

And my reference of past tense

Is only so I can keep my job

For it is in the hands of ventriloquists,

Or better yet,

It is in the hands of the puppets

We call politicians.

Vuka black man,

Phakama black woman,

Khuluma black child!

We are anything but free

From slavery and poverty,

Because if we were as free as the news says we are

101 poems about Things We Should Be Loud About

Your cousin would have been educated.

Your niece would have been employed last week,

And the rest of them, they would not be living in a toxic township.

Where the black man

Is not cheerful but envious

Of the success he couldn't acquire.

See, only God knows

When our time to

Flee the feisty pharaohs

Will come.

So we too, can build our Canaan.

Not this cheap overnight fantasy.

- Self-hate

101 poems about Things We Should Be Loud About

Let us not fall for the illusion

That we don't

Need a revolution.

The revolution written

In textbooks is only

The first page of a book we have yet to read.

So unless you are satisfied with the first page,

You should know that

There are more wars to be unravelled.

A lot of itches to be scratched.

And though they ought not to be staged like

The chaos we occasionally cause during protests,

101 poems about Things We Should Be Loud About

But we can use our pens as rifles,

Our lips and breath like nuclear,

And our hands as grand grenades.

- The Undone

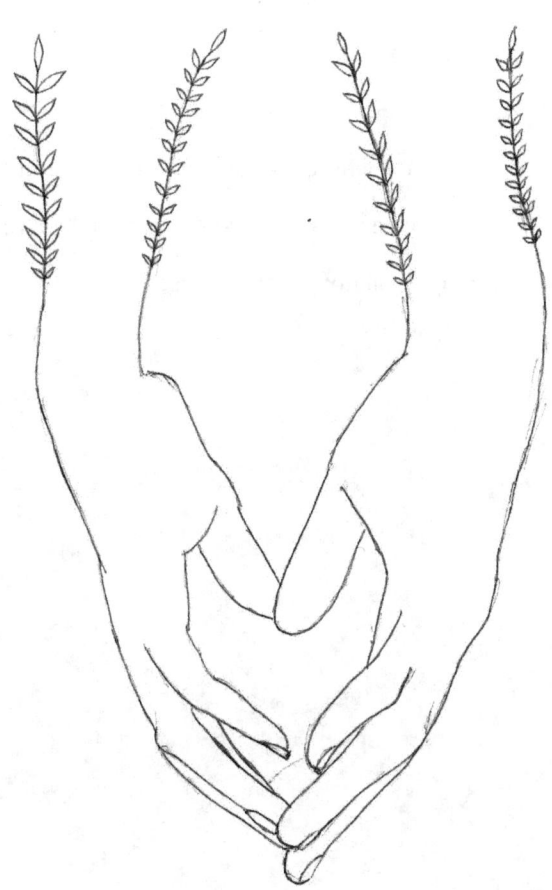

If you're tired of the fight,

Go stand at the back and heal

The wounded as the war has just begun.

For we cannot allow ourselves

To be forced into living in

A mental prison.

A place where we can't make a decision,

Because somehow we are told that we're depressed,

But in all honesty were just

Sick of being served a series

Of postponed promises

And unfinished dreams.

Half-truths and lovely lies.

We're sick of being served the same revolting meal,

You know, it was never meant to heal.

- Half-truths

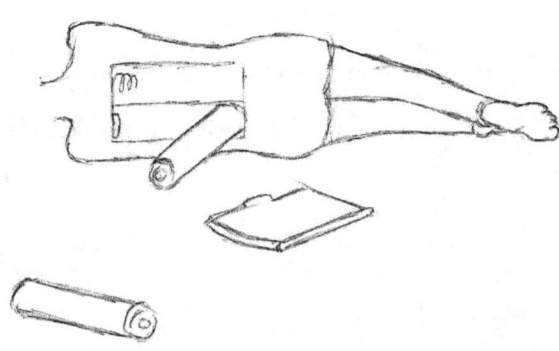

Let us live to like ash,

And pollute the world with melodies

Of hope and unshakable devotion,

Against the things we are

Forced to eat at the

Table of economic injustice.

Let us be a generation that vomits

Ideological indoctrination

In whatever form it serves.

Be resolute and

Concrete in what we believe.

Loud and aggressive with what we demand.

- Ashes

Our existence is birthed by the death of those before us.

Their sins, their victories.

How they loved, how they lived

And so will your life,

And the lives after yours.

So the idea that you

Should only live for yourself,

Is the alchemy of generational destruction and

Spiritual poverty.

Live for the future you'll never be in

Because ultimately you are the only one who'll carry tomorrow.

- Before Us

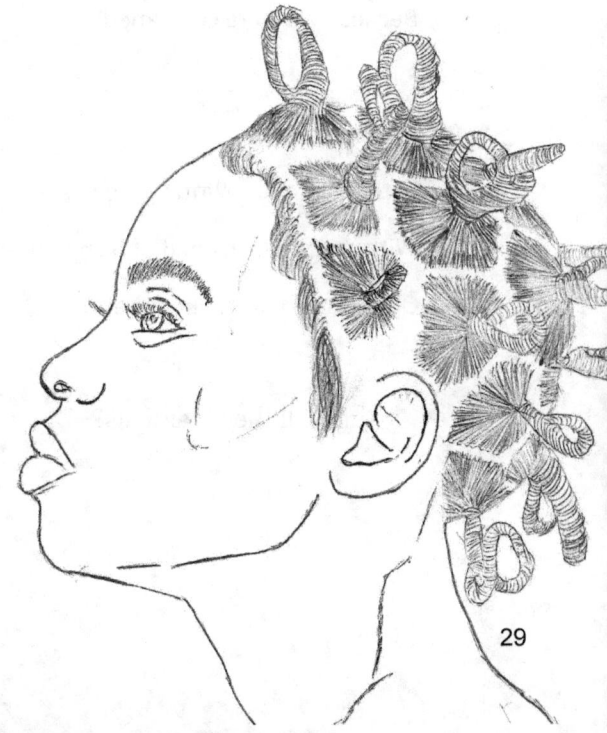

Our plea for freedom

Seems like a never-ending one.

As we are continuously

Stripped of what is ours –

So when we meet our end, we are

Left with nothing but bleeding hands

And a can of worms the size of an ocean.

It's sad how our children will blame us

For not standing up for the future

Because we were consumed

By trivial things

In the name of rewriting the past

With a caption, instead of fixing our eyes

On what is real and imminent.

- Will they blame us?

As long as we have not seen our

Words and works come into fruition.

We cannot claim victory nor gather

Harvest out of stubborn soil.

Wait for the rain, in whatever form it comes in.

Tears, terror, joy, or pure misery

Wait.

And teach yourself to do so without complaint,

- Waiting

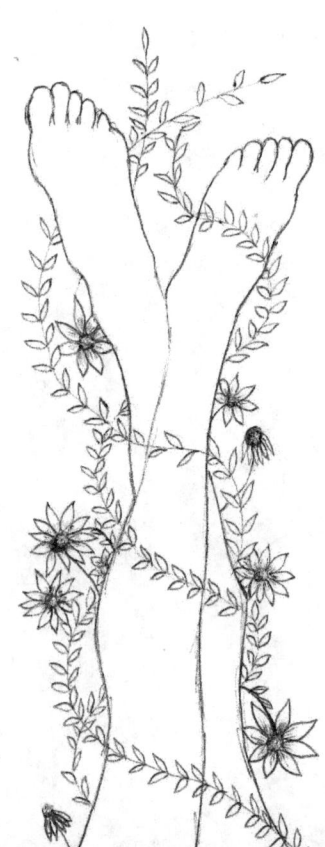

101 poems about Things We Should Be Loud About

As we eat the scraps left by the elite.

We should remember

That we are many and they are few,

And although it sometimes feels

Like they have more

Power over us,

And what we can and cannot do.

They are not God.

But we are God's people

And he can certainly see

How our land

Is being treated like an amputee

Even though our limbs are full and functioning

We're still given crutches coated with grudges.

Such is life for a man of colour.

- Table manners

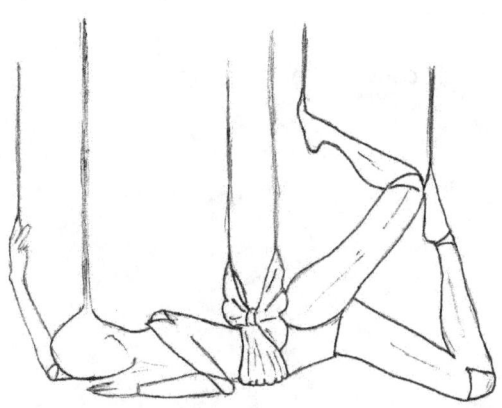

Africa is a baby drowning,

And we are the mother

Watching as the witness.

Fragile and bruised.

Wounded.

With sores pulsing and filled with pus.

Helpless but hopeful.

Even at the riverbank,

We still crawl and eat the dirt

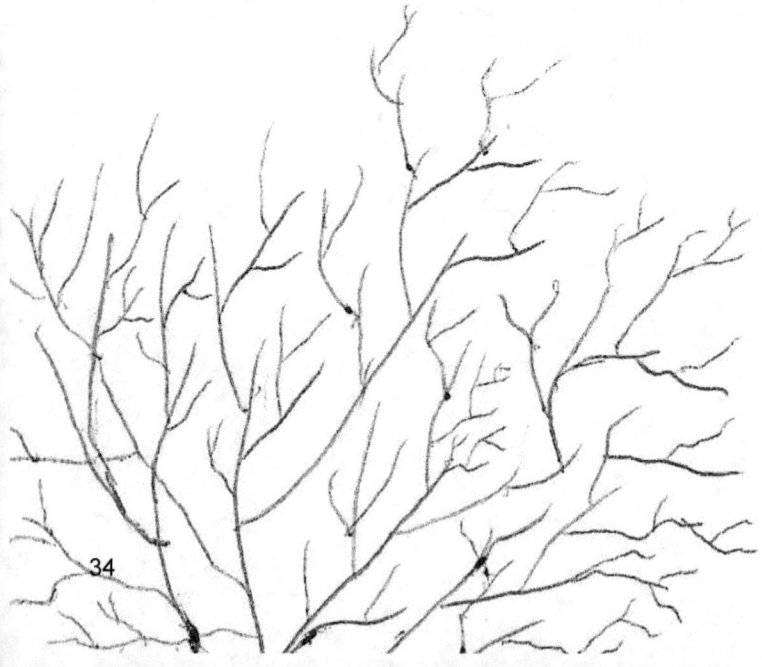

Because maybe,

That's all we have left.

Besides the dysfunctional wean

Drifting on our torn womb,

Breathing,

In spite of a throat filled with water.

- What a time to be alive

Speak

Until you are heard.

Until you are listened to,

In the face of fear, our words have the power to

Alter time, shake tomorrow,

And awaken the future.

Reform and revolt against

The people who serve you soil and sin.

Packaged in bundles of sunrises and

Sunsets that never end.

Half-broken promises,

And half-hearted apologies.

You cannot possibly accept the silence

Not now, not ever.

- A packaged sunrise

People coloured by the sun,

You are wired differently.

Don't forget that.

- A reminder

There is a child that's still confused as to

Which colour they should pick once

They've drawn a picture of themselves.

Between black and brown

Perhaps a jumble of both

Or a bit of everything.

While another,

Readily picks a crayon to

Colour match their tone,

The other is still debating

Why they are called black when

They're anything but black.

So if they start asking

Teach them who they are,

And why their tears are the sweat of their ancestors.

Tell them why the world is different for them.

Why their kings and queens were unwillingly

Turned into slaves and servants.

Tell them why they shouldn't allow

People to touch their hair,

And why their crowns are different.

Tell them that they are

The people of the soil, the people of the sun.

And that this land wouldn't survive without their breath.

Let them know that when it rains

They should not fear the thunder

But place their ear between the droplets

And listen for the voice of God.

A gentle whisper,

To let them know they matter.

- Crayons

Let us teach our minds to be unapologetic

And abandon taught patriarchy,

Along with the things written by

The pain of the past in our DNA.

Let us find something

Worth going to war for,

Worth fighting for,

Worth sacrificing for...

- Damned DNA

Breathe victory.

Even in the midst of defeat.

Do not allow your tongue to grow cold

Or your hands turn into stone.

Rebuke all uncertainty that comes with

The eye of the oppressor,

And follow through

With every idea,

Because ideas are a prophecy of your destiny.

A compass to the future.

To your future.

- Compass

Poverty is a living being.

He, she, they,

Are all from one race.

The black race.

The working class.

The ones that didn't afford to go to class.

Forced out of their own land

To live in places that

Make the eye itch and bleed.

Where pain is comfortable

Because there is nothing

Beyond it - only more suffering.

- Face of poverty

Don't fall for it, black man.

The solution to an

Already a rotten revolution.

And long empty speeches

With promises meant

To manipulate.

Emancipate yourself from

The slavery that comes with

Believing so-called leaders

Who bleed narcissism

And laugh in the face

Of great adversity.

- Still bleeding

Poverty is a tree that

Bears rotten fruit,

That government calls the economy.

An imbalance.

That causes nothing but endless suffering.

Rushing the great unwashed to their graves.

With politicians pretending to be the gardener.

Only to inject the soil

With poison,

Then cry when the fruit starts bleeding

While brushing bellies with,

The authors of white supremacy.

- It's in the soil

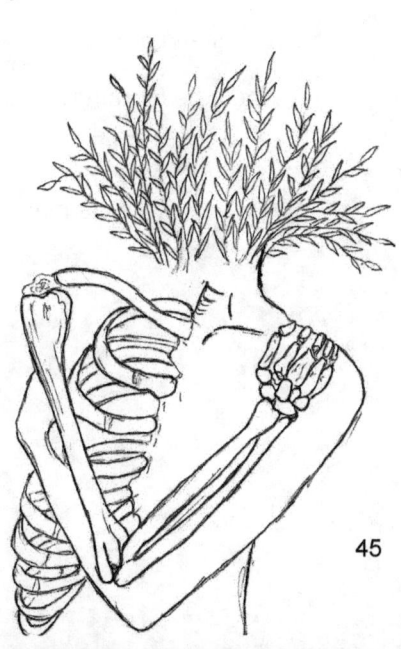

Keep your heart pure

For your household

But bitter for your country.

Dress your mind with

Knowledge and new perceptions.

Expose yourself to discomfort,

And never find satisfaction.

Moreover, pay no mind to any whisper

That creates any distraction to drift you from the cause.

Remain resilient

And stand beside every word you say.

Then the morning sun is yours to behold.

- Bitter beings

Let there be an unstoppable uprising

For the future

Of Africa amongst people of colour.

Don't let propaganda

Twist your mind to see

Your neighbour as the enemy.

When the greatest enemy is white supremacy.

The colour they don't want

You can see - but feel.

- For the sake of tomorrow

101 poems about Things We Should Be Loud About

Declare a new dawn

For the people who've

Carried our sunsets.

Conjure new beginnings

For the girl whose heart is

Fed by the fear of a broken man.

Awaken the men

That work till their sweat

Water the land.

Agitate the bones of

The woman that feel like

They've done it all.

Let them know their land

Is being sowed and harvested

By foreign hands…

- Not Yet Uhuru

101 poems about Things We Should Be Loud About

To be included is to be

Counted in,

Out of pity

And I don't want your pity

- No thank you

Our nation was forced to go into an ocean

With all these borrowed notions

And indoctrination motions.

To be washed of who we are,

And forget where we come from,

As if the soil on our skin was ever dirty.

- Borrowed notions

We have been engineered to

Kneel to whiteness,

Even though we were the ones

Brought into darkness

Just know that we see it,

In commercials, in sports, in courts,

At work, and even in aesthetics.

We feel it.

- Still kneeling

We cannot be a generation

Of living half a life.

Doing things half-heartedly.

Giving into the fear of living fully.

If we were to say truly

We are afraid of life's cruelties

A thin layer of skin

A mind with dreams yet too fragile

To begin and persevere regardless...

- Live intentionally

Do not be afraid to say no

And say it firmly

In places where the word needs to be heard.

Say it wholeheartedly for

An ambiguous refusal is

Only a weak acceptance.

A yes, in the eyes

Of those who willingly

Choose to oppress.

Do not be doubtful

Of your conscience and intuition

When it speaks.

Learn to amplify the voice inside you
Just enough so the one they hear
Will not sound doubtful.

Stand firm and true
To what the author of life
Has called you to be.

- No

It's the ability to bend and break

A bone in the present

For the future to flourish.

The urge to rise like the sun

As if it's not waiting for the

Moon to defeat it by nightfall.

That is will power.

That is what this life requires.

- Breaking bones

The truth is if we fear to do what is within us,

We fear our true selves.

Betraying the inner child

That was once told

You can be whatever you want to be.

- A debt to ourselves

101 poems about Things We Should Be Loud About

2

LOUDER THAN WORDS
The beginning of an end…

101 poems about Things We Should Be Loud About

The beginning of our tale

Only unfolds when we are peeled,

And bleeding untold sorrows,

Like the times we thought we'd met our end,

Or when the end times met us.

Where hope came too soon,

And we discovered that

Pain and loss have no timing.

That happiness fades

As quickly as it came.

As all else fails,

And sunsets become too slippery.

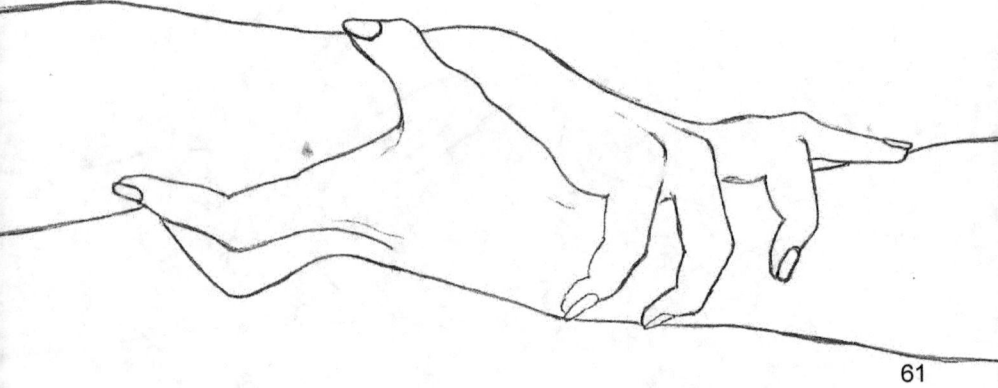

Finally, the gravel

Narrates our paths of

Where we fell and chose to rise again,

And so we should realise,

Our story never had a beginning

Nor will it ever have an end.

- Loose hands of time

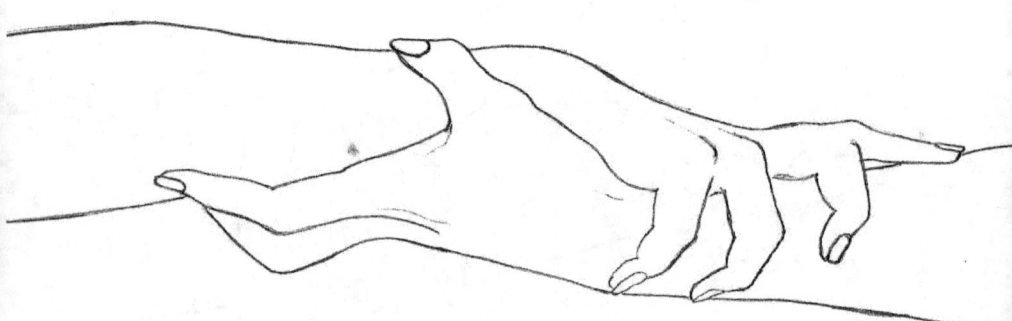

While destiny tells a story

Of the purpose

We're still seeking…

The sooner we realise that

The true essence of life

Lies in the sense we make of it.

It lies between the dark and light

Of the clouds at sunset.

In the butterfly that flew all the way to kiss your nose.

In the most traumatic things

That happens to the innocent.

And the best things that keep happening to the wicked.

I know it would be easier to be unbothered by these things,

But this life is anything but easy

In all aspects and perspectives.

For the poor and privileged

Are all met by the same end.

- Somehow the same

101 poems about Things We Should Be Loud About

When you set your mind on

A path far beyond

The mountains.

Do not waste your time looking

For carabiners and crampons,

Or a rope team of mountaineers.

Do it alone.

Do it with no apology,

No thought.

Immerse yourself in the journey,

And do not seek the sight of the end.

Even when in agony and annoyance,

Or euphoric ascendance.

Through it all, persevere with patience

Bearing within you only faith and mysticism.

- Unapologetic ascension

Our future selves wait for us.

Each morning, each day, each night.

Hoping that somehow,

We can shift our eyes

To the things above the

Mountain above us.

They wait,

For you to look past the pain

And gaze beyond the graze.

They are waiting for you to fall

And rise, time and time again,

For the ground belongs to us

As a place to fail

And in the end

A place to rest.

- Waiting for horizons

Do not close your mouth anymore,

When it comes to the things that

Have the most meaning to you,

For those are the things that

Build the world.

Those are the things that make you matter.

Speak the truth

With courage and stand by it.

Even if your voice cracks

Or your eyes fill with tears,

And someone laughs at the sound

Of your trembling tone.

Do not mind them,

For they clearly fail to understand the meaning of life.

The meaning of *your* life,

And the things you are called for.

Here on Earth, in this broken space.

You are the mender

Of whatever it is that sets your soul on fire.

- What you mean...

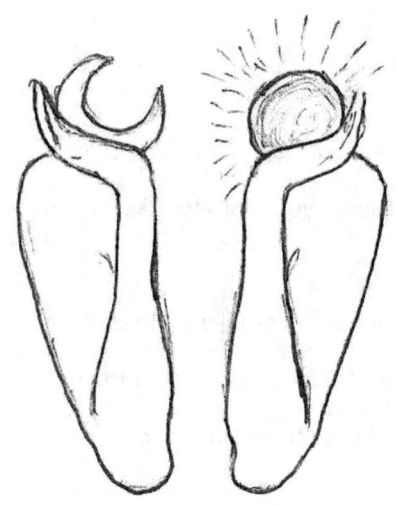

Stop - being timed and tempered

Towards the people and things

That makes you feel less alive.

Avoid submerging your soul

In necropolitics,

Because out of that ocean,

Spill only brine of bitterness, self-hatred

And waves of undeserved pride.

- Limited living

I see poetry written in your eyes

A marble of pain, happiness

And a bit of insanity.

Whether it's because of

How things are now.

A little bit out of place.

It's what drew me to you.

The will to carry on

Regardless of the missing pieces.

Because having it all together

Takes away the purpose of life

The spark, the reason...

- Out of place

We are the epitome

Of fast forward and rewind.

Living in the past and future

Slowly forgetting who we were

And constantly reminding ourselves

Who we want to be.

- Being and becoming

Ndi cela uxolo mtase khaya. *(I am asking for your forgiveness)*

I'm sorry,

On behalf of the people

That hurt you but don't know it,

Because you didn't

Mention the pain

And the tears that drained.

I know - the inside of you is dry,

There has been no rain.

You are a walking desert.

Your thoughts are like the sun.

Scorching unbearably

Above your mind.

Ndi cela uxolo sthandwa sam *(I'm sorry my love)*

I wish I could make you feel whole again,

But to be honest, you look better broken

Because now you're open,

And like a shattered mirror,

You reflect a rainbow.

Into bo nga kwazi uyenza *(something you would have never been able to do)*

Inhliziyo yakho ingo phukanga. (if your heart was never broken.)

But I will still apologise

Because maybe that's all you want to hear

I'm sorry, I'm sorry, I'm sorry.

Ndi cela uxolo mtase khaya *(I am asking for your forgiveness)*

Even if it's the last thing

You want to hear.

- Overdue apologies

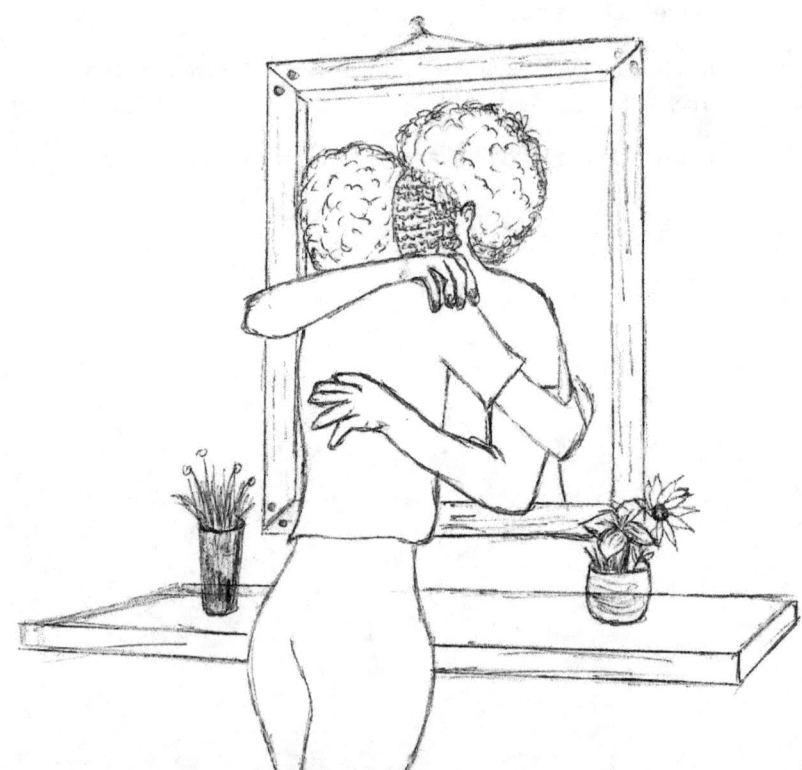

To those whose stories

Will never be heard or

Shared to the masses.

To those who've made an impact

In the shadows.

In the frontlines of silence.

To those building a life that will surely

Never fade in the minds of their witnesses

Who have never seen their weaknesses

Those who are rarely mentioned at

At the beginning or

The end of their story.

To me, you are all you need to be.

Not any less without the press.

No need to document a life fought for

Between sunrise and sunset

See, for you, it's a little more special.

- Wearing capes in the shadows

To us.

To those who know

        Our stories began before birth,

        And will continue

        Even when the ground

        Has swallowed us.

        We carry the earth,

        Its heartbeat and pieces

        From heartbreak.

        Below the surface of aches and blisters,

        Our cloudy hearts are called to pack

        In the burdens of pain to the other side of life.

- Carriers

We've taught ourselves how to

Escape the normal, and the occasional

Pouring of pain,

But when the rain falls

We don't run from it,

But towards it.

Praying that thunder forgets

Our stubborn feet,

That refuse to fall and remain fallen.

Even when our bones have been broken

By those our minds were tricked to trust.

- Thunder love

Sometimes justice feels

Like waiting for a lover

You know, will never come.

And the greatest pain

Is seeing time

Move on without the truth.

For the truth is a still being,

Patient but feisty,

Loving but reckless.

- Truth has its own timekeeper

When places you think you don't deserve to be in,

Call your name.

Do not shy away from the invitation,

Because I can assure you that it's something in you,

Something you can't see,

That's whispered your name.

In as much as

Wrong time, wrong place

Is rare,

And life is not always fair,

When it decides

To give and take as it pleases.

Be that as it may,

If you are moving towards the things

That make your eyes light up when you speak of them.

Then have no doubt,

You, my dear -

Are right where you need to be

- Longing for belonging

People like us shouldn't be asked how we're doing.

We should be asked how

We're even breathing,

Because if you were to be as honest as you should be.

You'd tell them how you're just getting by.

Going through the motions,

And it's not that you're complaining or ungrateful of life.

It's just that you haven't had enough time

To wrap your head around even being here,

Because suddenly you have an identity

A category, a race, a gender,

And you are somewhat defined

By the people who came before you.

As much as you try to rewrite the story

It always seems to erase itself,

In the eyes of a stranger

You could be a friend or danger.

Depending on the tombs of those before you

Their death is the beginning of your story

And so it continues for ages to come

- Same stranger

Everybody says you're going to be okay,

Or better yet it's the famous 'time heals' bullshit.

Yeah, bullshit.

Time makes it clear

That what you had has truly been lost.

It makes you realise

This world is a fucked up place

And that people are just ghosts with flesh,

Because we all disappear and reappear at some point, don't we?

What they should be saying instead is

What happens, happens

And even though you can't control most of it.

Enjoy it, indulge in it,

Yes - immerse yourself in it

Allow the pain, the love, the heartbreak,

The anger, the tears and

Everyone's favourite part to fake,

The happiness

Because time really doesn't care

Whether you heal or not, it simply does its deed,

As it has been for centuries…

It moves, and so should you.

- Ghosts with flesh

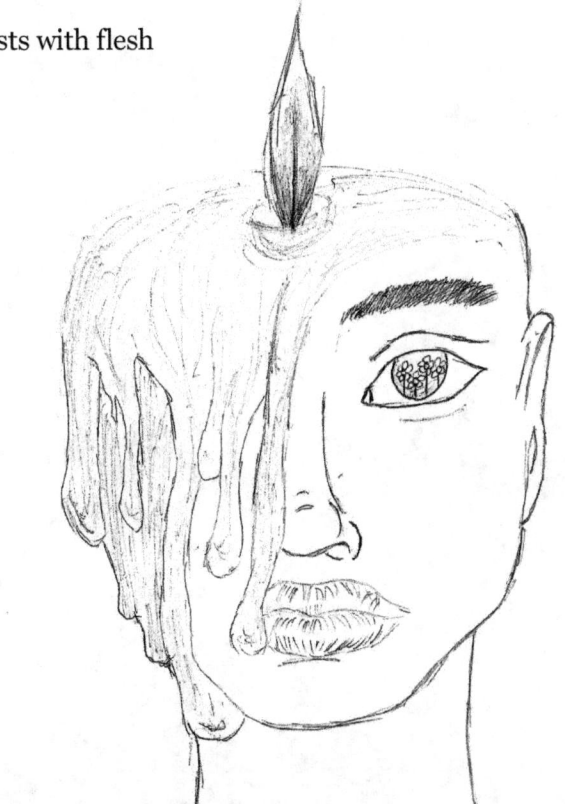

I can't write about you.

Even if I try to,

I always end up

Lost in the ellipsis you left me in.

You're that broken part of me

I know will never heal,

And quite frankly

I'm not waiting on anyone

Or anything to fix it.

Because it's ridiculous,

This reality

Without you in it.

Always In my head, in my heart,

In my dreams, but never where I need you to be.

Right here, next to me.

No ocean will ever cleanse

This anger, this pain, these salty tears

That fall - every time I think

A little too much about you,

And I only say it's too much

Because some seemed to have moved on

Just fine without you

But honestly I never will.

I'm not sure if I'm okay with that.

- Unforgotten

I cannot hold your hands so,

I'll hold on to the memory

Of how time stopped

When I was with you.

Constructing a memory

Of a place in my heart that

I can go when I miss you.

- Profound places

Today

I don't want to be sad

When I think of you,

Watching me

With not much to say

But I've learnt that it's okay...

I'd love to imagine

The hugging feeling and peace

That comes with your silence.

I don't want to think of the bad days

And wish they never happened

Rather resurrect our silly differences.

Only to embrace their existence

In the past and present.

In the mind and heart.

I want to reform your image

In this moment

As if you weren't as

Near and far as you are.

I'd like to think

That you hear my thoughts and dreams

Echo through space and time…

- Between you and I

Familiar feeling

101 poems about Things We Should Be Loud About

The truth is

We are all here

To disappear.

Like the wind,

We come and go.

Remembered then - slowly forgotten.

Then we all become a story

Combined with

The time we lived in,

And, the things we loved

Along with the

Great things we did.

What we stood up for,

The things we died for

The things we were supposed to fight for,

And all the battles we won and lost,

In our time.

At that point you'll just be another name in a history book.

- Another name

It's not time we have a race against

But what our past selves have been

Waiting for, crying for and bleeding for.

It's the late night talks

With the shadow of death.

Pleading him for another gamble

To meet our destined selves.

- You and I before...

You should go out more.

See unfamiliar faces and

Do things that make you feel uncomfortable.

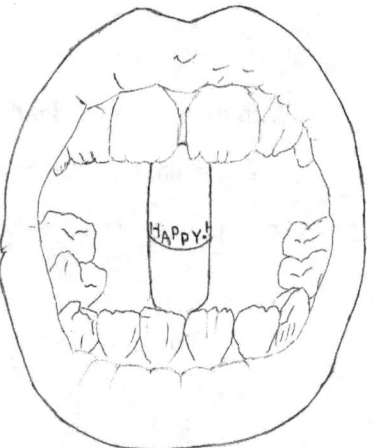

Do the things that you love.

The things that give you some sense of purpose,

And make time evaporate.

Those are the things we live for,

And perhaps even die for.

- To live for, to die for...sweet life

It gets lonely,

When you remove yourself from people,

When the soul craves silence.

Be as it may, do not let the hollowness fool you.

Fill it with the sounds your inner child craves for.

Do things

That makes you feel alive.

- Hollow times

Is all the fear worth it?

Behold, the greatest fear should not lie

In the things we want to become.

Nevertheless, we should tremble

At the thought of

What we don't want to become,

And falling into the pit of death

Without having done

What we are called for.

- A calling

Even a child can tell when a storm is on its way,

And the skies grow bitter

Groaning like a woman birthing.

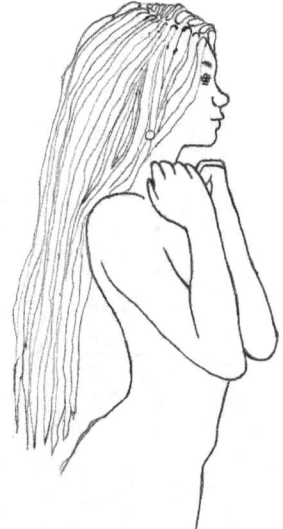

Above says: 'land behold'

A wreckage is coming

And the ground has nowhere to hide.

All the trees and great mountains

Have to abide to the storm

Knowing it's beginning but not its end.

We are the trees and great mountains

Allowing the rain to fall when

The time has come we do anything but run.

- Abiding by the storm

Like Abraham,

Keep sacrificing.

That extra hour of sleep.

The night out you know you don't need.

Do it.

Sacrifice, for the sake of tomorrow,

For who you want to be.

Do it for them.

- Doing it for tomorrow

101 poems about Things We Should Be Loud About

Isn't it strange how

We sometimes

Find comfort in the

Things that hurt us most?

- Isn't it?

101 poems about Things We Should Be Loud About

3

BREAKING THE MOULD
Can You Challenge the Status Quo in Today's World?

101 poems about Things We Should Be Loud About

Dear dark skinned, multi coloured eye, freckled, broken human

It's time to pick up the pieces,

We got lost on the way to putting our inner child in the closet.

A new dawn has come for the voiceless

An awakening that is undefeated.

Even though we are still crawling.

Our becoming has finally begun

The heavens have heard our desperate cry,

And collected our tears…

At the park by the bench,

In the car, in the bathroom at work…

At school, even at home, in the hallway, in the kitchen,

On the couch.

Also on your bed, on your favourite

Pillow that you spend nights sobbing into.

Even on days when it doesn't feel like it.

The warrior in you is stronger than ever,

Your healing has begun

The end is in sight.

- The beginning of an end

Let me give you a new definition of perfect.

Firstly, perfect is not white.

Lastly, there is no such thing as perfect.

In skin colour, in body form, in everything,

There has to be a little bit of ugly

In between all the pretty.

A little bit of war, for love to find its purpose,

A little bit of darkness,

For light to be seen.

Perhaps more tears and tears

For the long-awaited opening,

And a bit of broken, for mending to happen.

101 poems about Things We Should Be Loud About

So if you ever looked for perfect

Know that it looks unfinished,

And still trying.

- The in-betweens

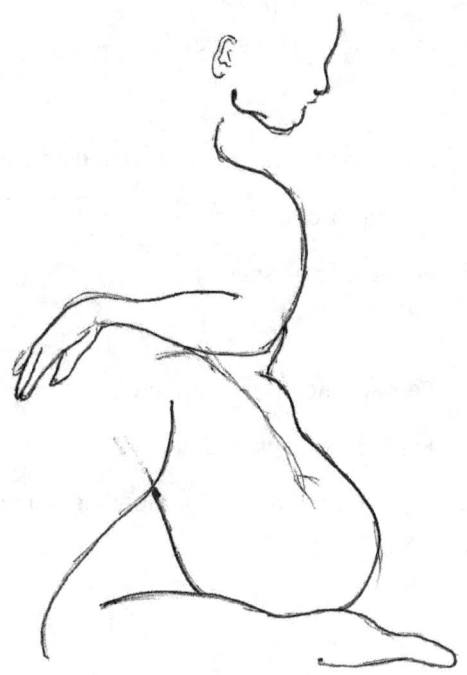

If courage be but little.

Allow the mind to remind the heart

Of where this defeated body has been.

Bent, broken and bruised.

Dragged down the dirty dumps

Of dainty daunting hearts,

That owe you nothing.

Not even a plea of forgiveness,

Nor unruly explanations filled with

A bunch of 'I'm sorries'

And sugar coated apologies.

Fed forcefully from their minds and lips

Trying to articulate stitches to fix your heart

That almost instantly, vomit words

That came too late.

- Empty apologies

Some people aim for the sky

Others aim for the stars.

Then there's us,

We aim for anything beyond the universe.

- Above usual

When you pass

Even the wind listens

And wraps itself around you.

Maybe that's why people stare,

In awe of what

You bare,

Or maybe there's just something

Between your teeth,

Or you walk a bit wobbly.

Perhaps you have a

Peculiar way of

Dressing your body.

Either way,

You caught their attention

And although they might not go to bed thinking about you.

Your passing existence

Is an experience worth obsessing about,

Even if it's for a few seconds.

- Existing

The biggest climate crisis

Is the one I see when I

Look into the eyes

Of a being that's lost all hope.

The tides and troubles

Have taken their stride...

You look hollow, but isn't it incredible

That the breath in you still remains

Still, daring to live.

- Breath and body

On days when looking

In the mirror

Becomes an investigation,

Of how the lines turned into wrinkles,

And teary times seem to have made their bed

Underneath your eyes.

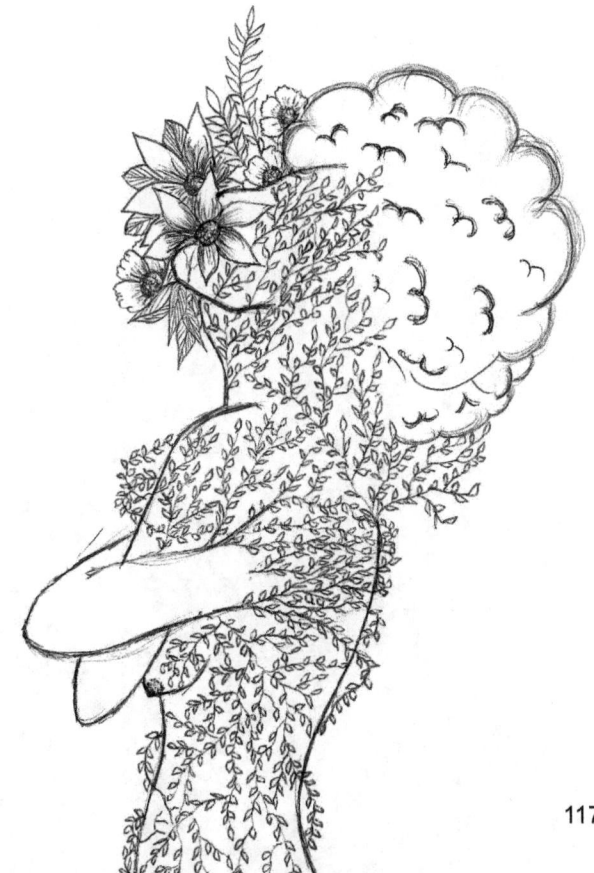

Think of your body as a book that tells

A story of where it has been.

What it has seen in flesh and mind.

Scriptures of happiness, madness, and sadness

And all the little things that we can never retell but

Keep between ourselves and the soul we see in the mirror...

- Body scriptures

Somewhere between the

Reasons for pain and loss

Lies an illusion of continuity,

And a mind that is forgetful,

With a heart that refuses to admit

That with time things do change…

Somewhere between the

Reasons for pain and loss

Lies an illusion of continuity,

And a mind that is forgetful,

With a heart that refuses to admit

That with time things do change…

- Changing seasons

Time has shaped our identities

It still is.

Now as we breathe.

Beneath the same skies,

Our ancestors searched

For answers,

With them now below us.

Bearing the beat of our feet

Soaking the salt of our tears.

Holding pieces of our hearts

We forgot to pick up when it was shattered,

Time and time again.

In the well of their blood dwells

Our deepest desires

And the things our lips refuse to utter…

The things we don't want to talk about

Or the things we hope others have

Forgotten or not forgotten.

Perhaps the things burned

Into the core of our souls,

Rejecting our constant plea to leave our thoughts.

- Searching

101 poems about Things We Should Be Loud About

This body is your home,

For as long as you are here.

Furnish it with beautiful dreams.

Paint it with hope.

Strengthen it with valour,

And whenever you come across its reflection

Smile, and admire its imperfections.

Love how different it is from all the others.

Embrace your existence in it, for as long as you can.

And when you invite a guest

Put them next to an open door

Because people come and go

And at the end of it all

You are, once again, left alone…

- Open doors

And when you think

Align your thoughts,

Like a compass point them

In the path you seek.

- A seeker's thoughts

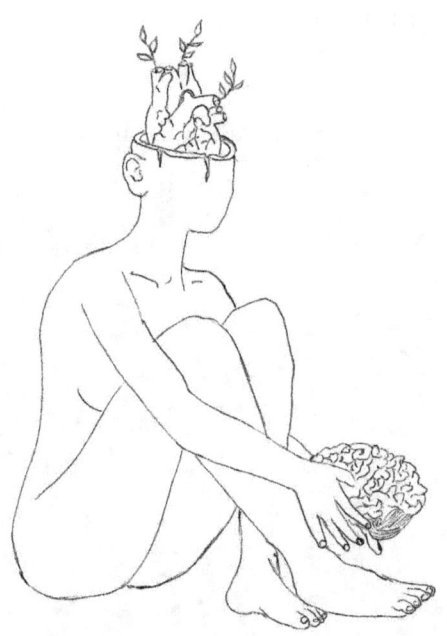

Sometimes the feeling is so overwhelming

That words can't explain,

And that's okay.

To just feel.

Because not everything needs expensive words and explanations.

Just a moment in the mirror.

Head tilting, eyes filling.

Then, silence.

- Moments in the mirror

Disappointment is only

Created by expectation of our reality,

Furnished by things that mean

Something to us

But nothing to others.

- Nothing to you

Remain in the light.

Even when darkness wraps itself around you,

Cease the desires that come with it.

Along with the things that make

Your soul feel heavy, and your eyes rain.

Furthermore, avoid adjusting the brightness to

Justify the eyes of those that say you blind them,

And abide in your kind of luminescence.

- A different light

It was hard to get here.

It sometimes seemed impossible.

The thought of the future.

The big, scary, risky, unpredictable future.

A place we all know we're meant to arrive,

But somehow we're still

Caught off guard when we do,

And we still will.

Even if it leads us to our death.

It somehow makes life

A little worth watching,

Because unlike the movie

We didn't see the trailer

And maybe that is what

Makes it unusual…

When we see ourselves age

Beyond the stage we thought we wouldn't,

The future doesn't seem so impossible anymore.

- Still here

Life is patient.

Slow and gradual.

It's time we'll have to convince,

To not be in such a rush

For our bodies to sleep in a pit.

- *Quick sleep*

Oh and sometimes we don't want to be broken

But it's brokenness we come from.

Relentless cries from our mothers as we left the womb.

So why expect any less from this life?

- *An escape*

Yellow grass is still called grass.

No one analyses its incapabilities

And says, "cut this grass"

For everyone in the right mind knows

It's just waiting for winter to pass,

The rain to pour, and the sun to shine.

Why can't you wait for the rain?

When you look in the mirror

Why do you say "I hate this place"

Why do you sound so hopeless?

Why can't you wait for the sun?

The break of a new dawn.

Why not be like the watchmen in Isaiah?

Standing firm in reminding God,

Even though he does not forget.

- *The watchmen*

Learn to live in your body

Without apologising for its existence.

This is the space

That your soul has to occupy.

For as long as you're here

The inside matters just as much as the outside.

And you have no right

To let people who live on the outside hurt the inside.

You are the gatekeeper

Of your peace.

So from today

Be unapologetic.

Because time

Is still bowing to your existence.

    - *The temple*

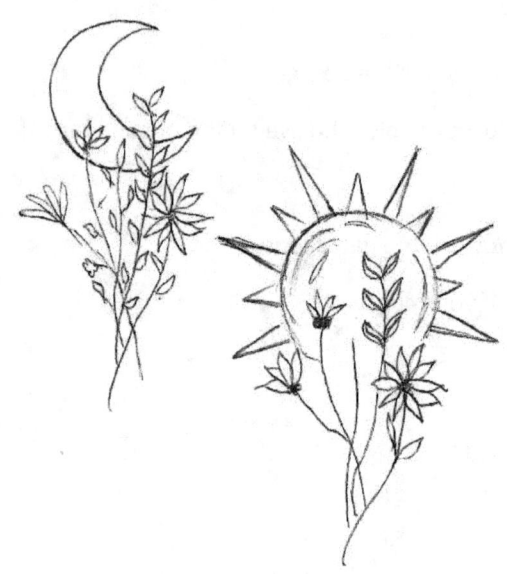

The sooner we see our bodies

As nothing, but mere vessels

Of the greater God within us,

Than slaves of culture, religion, and necropolitics.

Maybe we'd be less bothered,

By the gap between our thighs,

The darkened underarms, the stretch marks, the weight,

The height, the skinny, the curvy, the thick

The mole, the freckle, the wrinkle, the pimple, the dimple,

This life we live would be a lot simpler,

And perhaps we'd become

A little more unapologetic

Of what these vessels

Are capable of.

- *Perfect imperfections*

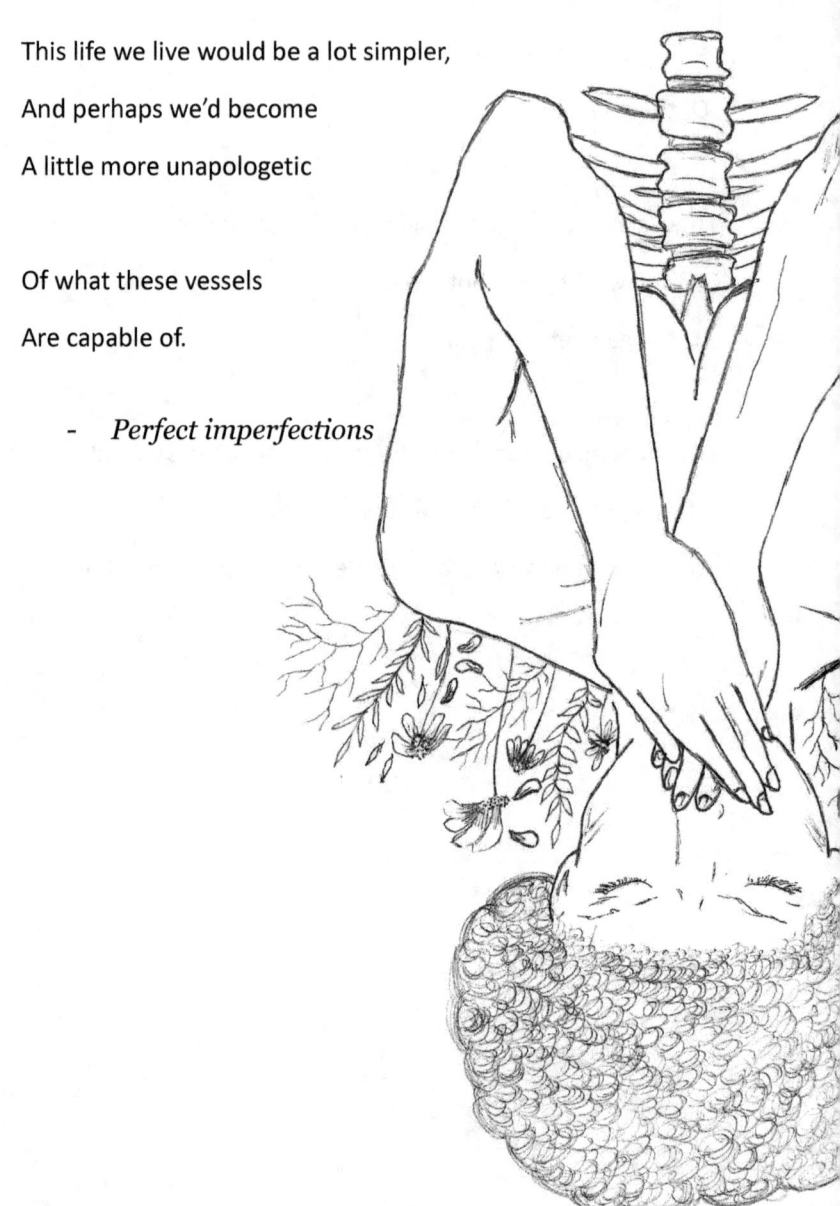

Before you drown yourself

In expensive fairy tales,

And empty promises.

Know that the world

Does not expect that

Much effort from you.

Not the diamonds and pearls,

Nor the blood-sculpted body,

Or even the rough around the edges body.

Just a body with a soul

That finds peace in the simplest things…

- *Expectations*

101 poems about Things We Should Be Loud About

4.

REVELATIONS AND DECEPTIONS
A Confrontation to Rape, False Prophets, and the Divine Paradox

101 poems about Things We Should Be Loud About

101 poems about Things We Should Be Loud About

I was told to write about rape.

Men who beat their wives.

Father's that are absent,

And mothers that left their wombs in the delivery room.

But to be honest,

These people are all the same

The rapist, the killer, and the soul terrorist.

They're all broken people,

Veins flowing with glass.

Scratching and tearing the walls of their soul,

And an inner child crying silently for help

In the wrong places

While finding comfort amongst wicked faces.

Because the church has been closed,

And claimed by unlawful judges,

And priests with dirty hands,

And dainty hearts.

Sniffing papers out of poor pockets

Harvesting from vineyards that

They never ploughed in…

- *Soul terrorists*

Why does it make sense

To hate a person you

Once loved dearly?

Is it the disappointment of your expectations?

Is it finally facing the reality

You refused to believe?

Perhaps it may be

Unwrapping their mummified

Secrets and uncovering

The things that make

Them sleepless and the

Things that make up their uniqueness

It's their form of brokenness.

And then you wonder

If it's what called you to them.

Silently but distinctly

In their eyes

Either a cry for help

Or a bloodthirsty roar...

- *Unloving*

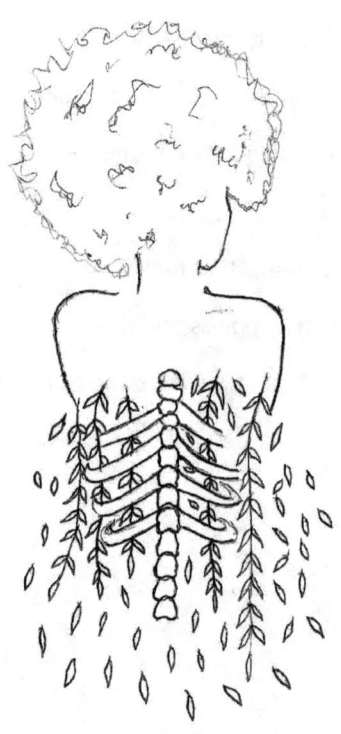

The sooner we realise

The wars within

Are the birth of all external wars,

We'll spend less time

Praying for sanctuaries

And weeping for centuries

In a world where peace is a foreign language,

Too hard to teach

Beings that cried at birth.

- *The sooner the better*

How do you spot a weak being?

Almost like in a supermarket,

Perfectly packaged

With promises way above 'too good to be true'

No flaws, no cracks - almost holy.

Yet with eyes sinking into yours, speaking highly of themselves.

Too pretty to pet,

Too confident to pretend,

Too dangerous to predict.

See a weak being

Will give out sweet fear like

Candy on Halloween.

While waiting for you to taste it,

Feel it, submit to it,

Bend down and worship it.

Lift your skirt and pray to it

Your body begs to forget it.

The smell of their weakness.

Hidden beneath their bones.

A broken soul and crippled mind.

The devil's masterpiece.

- *Almost holy*

A crushed spirit utters

Only words with venom

That cripple and kill,

Dreams of souls

Once cheerful and pure

With eyes like blossoms.

I've seen

Dead souls speak of a life and light

Too far and out of sight.

- *Church*

If you're the kind

That hurts good people.

The kind that intentionally causes pain.

Just know, that you will spend your days

Eating broken glass and stone,

In the corner with the devil.

Though I don't wish you any harm.

See that you know,

But I do wish upon you what you deserve.

It's just a rule of life

You should never make

A good heart bleed.

- *I wish you no harm*

Then there are those

That live in the unseen

But love the scene

Of water aggressively filling your eyes.

Those who patiently wait

For the final blink

So the ink

Of the words they've written on your heart

Can trickle on the cheeks that seldom forget

How to blow up and smile from time to time.

   - *A reminder to smile*

The earth is still full of rocks

So pick one up

And trust it instead,

Of standing

On shaky beliefs,

Crafted by beings who would never

Be able to comprehend,

What a day is like in your universe.

- *Shaky beliefs*

All women are gold diggers.

All men are psychopathic cheaters.

That is the headline of this generation.

The birth of a new kind of evil and

The unwavering desire to cease

All earth has to offer.

Without ever having

To sweat for it or

Spend nights praying for it.

Simply swipe and submerge

Yourself in all the things

You'll die without.

Oh what a sad generation.

- *Unceasing*

Pay great attention to those who advocate for life,

And walk around in

Glad rags and black ties.

The people who want to be greeted first,

So you can quench their constant

Thirst for validation.

They have the best seats and

Almost, the best lives.

The biggest smiles and the loudest laugh,

But in the unseen

They're souls like ghosts with hollow stomachs

Devoured from within.

- *False advocates*

Praise be to God

The living God.

Praise be to God

In the storm, in serenity,

In life, in death

In misery, in tranquillity

In war, in peace

In failure, in victory

In clarity, in opacity

In love, in love, in love…

- *A praise*

When you meet the tempest

Greet him firmly

Like a guest you've heard has

Plotted wicked deeds against you.

Wash his feet,

And serve him food

Like you would with royalty,

For our greatest revelations

Come not from the bearer of happiness

But from the things that flood our pillows,

Leave our hearts swollen and eyes inflated.

- *The guest*

When you're engulfed, with what feels

Like endless suffering and pain,

With no end in sight

And time folds into itself once again.

Call to mind,

That God's clock is different,

It's unpredictable, and maybe that's

What makes it worth believing in,

Because who likes predictable things?

- *A different clock*

I hope I'm the reason you cry,

When life finally unravels itself

And you meet vultures and creatures

With a heart unmatched to the one you gave me.

You'll remember

That I existed in your lifetime

And didn't leave even when it was night time

I still choose to be the sun against the moon.

- *The reason*

A broken soul looks like poetry.

A lonely mind sounds like music.

In a crowd of this life's travellers

See how wide the smile of

A shattered heart looks like

A tsunami.

Disastrous beauty from far

But humming death when near.

- *The humming*

www.ingramcontent.com/pod-product-compliance
Lightning Source LLC
Chambersburg PA
CBHW072005290426
44109CB00018B/2140